BACK2BACK!

The Georgia Bulldogs Repeat as National Champions

Book design by Josh Crutchmer

Photos courtesy of AP Images

ISBN: 978-1-957005-09-6

Printed in the United States of America

Twice as Nice!

Georgia Coach Kirby Smart was part of college football's greatest dynasty as an assistant for Nick Saban at Alabama and now he has launched his own.

After going through the Crimson Tide last season to win Georgia's first national title in 41 years, the top-ranked Bulldogs did it again with an impressive victory over a talented TCU team. The rest of the college football world is trying to keep up with a Georgia program that has a 29-1 record the past two years with a pair of College Football Playoff titles. A dynasty by any definition. That the Bulldogs had an NFL record 15 players drafted last April only adds to the heft of their latest achievement.

Georgia becomes the first school to repeat as champs in major college football since Alabama a decade ago, and the first to go back-to-back in the nine-year history of the four-team playoff.

With a blueprint similar to Saban's but modified to fit Georgia, Smart has built a program that appears capable of accomplishing the ultimate goal: sustained excellence.

"It has taken lot of hard work, a standard, a belief in the culture within it," Smart said about his program's two year run of success. "I think each and every year you have a different team so you have to wipe the slate clean and try to redraw the art piece with what you've got. Fortunately, we were able to get it done this year."

Georgia fans everywhere are happy they did.

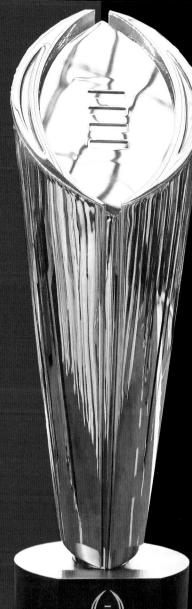

NATIONAL
CHAMPIONSHIP

PRESENTED BY

Georgia quarterback Stetson Bennett holds the trophy as his teammates celebrate defeating TCU 65-7 at SoFi Stadium for the national championship.

No Doubt About It

Top-Ranked Georgia Rolls TCU, 65-7, to Lock Up Second National Title in a Row.

January 9, 2023

NGLEWOOD, Calif. — Stetson Bennett flashed a wry grin as he walked off the field, stopping to hug coach Kirby Smart as the crowd roared.

It was all standing ovations and sideline snacks in the fourth quarter of college football's most lopsided title game.

In emphatic and overwhelming fashion, Georgia became the first team to repeat as College Football Playoff national champions and left no doubt the 'Dawgs are the new bullies on the block.

Bennett threw two touchdown passes and ran for two scores in the first half as No. 1 Georgia demolished No. 3 TCU 65-7 Monday night.

The Bulldogs (15-0) are the first repeat champs in major college football since Alabama went back-to-back a decade ago. There appears to be a new dynasty emerging from the Southeastern Conference.

"We wanted our kids to play without fear," Smart said. "All year I told them, I said, 'We ain't getting hunted guys, we're doing the hunting, and hunting season's almost over. We've only got one more chance to hunt,' and we hunted tonight."

TCU (13-2), the first Cinderella team of the playoff era, never had a chance against the Georgia juggernaut. Unlike Michigan in the Fiesta Bowl semifinal, the Bulldogs would not succumb to the Hypnotoads' spell.

Georgia turned in one of the all-time beatdowns in a big game, reminiscent of Nebraska running over Florida by 38 in the 1996 Fiesta Bowl, USC's 36-point rout of Oklahoma in the 2005 Orange Bowl and Alabama's 28-point BCS blowout over Notre Dame in 2013.

But this was worse.

Too much talent. Too well-coached. Two straight titles for the 'Dawgs.

No team has ever scored more points in a national championship game, dating to the beginning of the BCS in 1998.

With 13:25 left in the fourth quarter, Smart called timeout in the middle of an offensive drive so Bennett could exit to hero's ovation in the final game of his circuitous college career.

"That was special," said Bennett, who finished 18 for 25 for 304 yards and four touchdown passes. "I'll remember that for the rest of my life."

Georgia offensive linemen were munching on chicken wings on the sideline as the game wound down. Then, for the second straight year, the Bulldogs were showered by confetti and presented a championship trophy.

"I love this team, I love those fans, I love our band. I love everybody," Bennett said during the presentation ceremony. "Back-to-back, baby. Back-to-back."

Smart is now 81-15 in his first seven seasons at Georgia with two national titles. His mentor, Alabama coach Nick Saban, was 79-15 with three titles in his first seven seasons with the Tide.

The Bulldogs were a different kind of dominant this season: not quite as stingy on defense, but more explosive on offense.

Earlier in Smart's tenure at his alma mater, Georgia fans worried about whether the

Georgia offensive lineman Xavier Truss lifts quarterback Stetson Bennett after Bennett ran for a touchdown in the first half of the College Football Playoff championship win over Texas Christian.

former defensive coordinator for Saban would be able to build an offense to match this high-scoring era of college football.

Under third-year coordinator Todd Monken, the Bulldogs have become prolific, creative and diverse offensively. They picked apart TCU's 3-3-5 defense from all angles.

Versatile tight end Brock Bowers had seven catches for 152 yards. Receiver Ladd McConkey caught two TDs. Georgia ran for 254 yards with seven players gaining at least 10.

The Bulldogs scored all six times they touched the ball in the first half. Twice Bennett ran it in himself; the former walk-on turned two-time national champion was barely touched on the two quarterback keepers.

He hit a wide-open McConkey for a 34-yard score in the first quarter, a perfectly executed play out of a bunched formation that had TCU's defensive backs in disarray. Bennett's 22-yard score to Adonai Mitchell was a higher degree of difficulty, dropped in over a defender who had tight coverage.

It looked a lot like the Bennett-to-Mitchell touchdown that gave Georgia a fourth-quarter lead it would not relinquish against Alabama in last year's CFP title game.

Georgia vanquished the Tide to break a 41-year national title drought last season, avenging its only regular-season loss in the process.

There was no such drama against the upstart Horned Frogs.

"The journey was great. It's something I'll never forget," TCU running back Emari Demercado said. "Obviously, didn't end how we wanted it, but at the end of the day this journey was something great."

Bulldogs wide receiver Ladd McConkey hauls in a first-half touchdown during a national championship win over TCU.

This year the Bulldogs never had to worry about Alabama. They rolled through the SEC, survived Ohio State in a classic CFP semifinal and then completed a perfect season with an historic blowout.

Bennett hit Bowers for a 22-yard score with 10:52 left in the third quarter to make it 45-7. The sophomore from Northern California signaled touchdown while lying on the turf at Sofi Stadium. Bennett smiled as he tapped helmets with one of his linemen.

Georgia's famous bulldog mascot UGA could not make cross-country trip to root on his team, but it still felt a little like Sanford Stadium in SoCal.

Many of the TCU fans cleared out with more than half the fourth quarter left, choosing to venture out into a rainy and chilly night rather than watch any more of the massive mismatch.

Heisman Trophy runner-up Max Duggan threw two first-half interceptions in the final game of his roller-coaster TCU career.

A four-year starter who never played in a bowl before this season, Duggan led TCU on one of the most improbable runs in college football history.

Unranked after a losing 2021 season and picked seventh in the Big 12 for Sonny Dykes' first year as coach, the Frogs won nine games by 10 or fewer points. They were within a victory of the program's first national title since 1938.

But they ran into monster.

"As long as you don't have entitlement in your program, you've got a shot," Smart said. "And right now, we don't have that."

Georgia running back Kendall Milton (2) celebrates a touchdown run against TCU during the first half.

Bulldog defensive back Javon Bullard intercepts a pass intended for TCU receiver Derius Davis during the first half of Georgia's national-title victory.

Georgia tight end Brock Bowers hauls in a second-half touchdown catch against TCU safety Abraham Camara.

Georgia linebacker
Jalon Walker sacks TCU
quarterback Max Duggan
during the second half of
the national championship.

Georgia quarterback Stetson Bennett (13) celebrates victory over TCU on the field at SoFi Stadium after the national title game.

Not Missing a Beat

Bennett,
Defense
Put on a
Show for
Defending
Champs
in Rout of
Oregon.

September 3, 2022

ATLANTA — Stetson Bennett and the Georgia defense picked up where they left off in last year's national championship game, even with a bunch of their former teammates now playing in the NFL.

Bennett threw for 368 yards and accounted for three touchdowns, a revamped defense didn't miss a beat, and the No. 3 Bulldogs looked very much like a champion intent on repeating with a 49-3 rout of No. 11 Oregon on Saturday.

Bennett completed 25-of-31 passes with two touchdowns and ran for another score in the season opener before calling it a day in the third quarter. By that point, Georgia led 42-3 and had thoroughly ruined the debut of Oregon coach Dan Lanning.

Georgia really opened it up on offense, throwing 37 times for 439 yards.

"I think when you watch what they did today, if you're watching from home, you're saying, 'Man, I'd love to come play in that offense,'" coach Kirby Smart said.

After spending the last three years as Georgia's co-defensive coordinator, Lanning got a look at his former team from the opposing sideline in a game played before a predominantly red-clad crowd at the home of the NFL's Atlanta Falcons.

He saw just how far the Ducks have to go.

"That locker room is hurting a little bit," Lanning said. "But they're ready to grow."

Bennett, the former walk-on who led a storybook run to Georgia's first national title since 1980, returned for a sixth college season with a firm grip on the starting job after battling for playing time most of his career.

Bennett was the offensive MVP of both Georgia victories in last year's College Football Playoff. He started his final season with a career high for passing yards.

"It's always good to go in being the guy," Bennett said. "It was pretty cool."

He guided the Bulldogs to the end zone on all six possessions he played. He ran for a 1-yard score and tossed TD passes of 4 yards to Ladd McConkey — spinning away from a pass rusher who appeared to have him corralled — and 18 yards to Adonai Mitchell.

There were some questions about the Georgia defense, which had five players off the 2021 unit selected in the first round of the NFL draft.

Any doubts were quickly put to rest by a swarming group that looked very much like last year's defense for the ages, making life miserable for new Oregon quarterback Bo Nix.

"One of our mottos is, 'No one in our end zone,'" said Christopher Smith, who had one of Georgia's two interceptions.

Nix transferred to Eugene after starting at Auburn the last three seasons. He immediately found himself facing a team he lost to three times while playing in the SEC.

Make it 0-4.

Nix's frustration was evident when he buried his helmet in his hands after a false-start penalty.

Georgia's day was epitomized by a short pass to Darnell Washington that turned into a big gain when the 6-foot-7, 270-pound tight end shrugged off one defender hitting him high and hurdled another who tried to bring him down low.

Georgia running back Kendall Milton is lifted up after rushing for a touchdown against Oregon in the season opener.

Georgia's Darnell Washington
hurdles Oregon's Bryan Addison
during the Chick-fil-A Kickoff Game

Former Georgia head coach Vince Dooley is honored for his birthday before the game against Oregon.

Samford Overmatched

Defense
Stars in
Shutout
of FCS
Opponent.

September 10, 2022

ATHENS — A shutout win wasn't enough for a No. 2 Georgia coming off its impressive opener when it scored touchdowns on its first seven offensive possessions.

The reigning national champions fell short of that lofty standard against FCS Samford.

Stetson Bennett still passed for 300 yards while throwing and running for touchdowns and No. 2 Georgia's rebuilt defense delivered another dominant performance in the Bulldogs' 33-0 win on Saturday.

One week after giving up only a field goal in a 49-3 rout of then-No. 11 Oregon, Georgia (2-0) held Samford (1-1) to 128 yards and three first downs.

The offense, however, settled for four field goals — including on its first two possessions after moving the ball inside Samford's 10.

"We didn't score touchdowns," Georgia coach Kirby Smart said." ... You come off a week like Oregon where every opportunity to score a touchdown, we score a touchdown. And then we take a huge step back and have to kick field goals. Good teams, you can't do that. You have to be able to execute well. ... We have to do a better job."

Bennett completed 24 of 34 passes, including a 3-yard scoring pass to freshman Dillon Bell. Even so, he wasn't satisfied.

"I think we're all upset we didn't execute as well as we could have in the first half," Bennett said, adding "Too many field goals."

There were no complaints on defense, where Georgia has reloaded after losing eight players in this year's NFL draft, including five in the first round. Overall, Georgia had a record 15 players taken in the draft.

One year ago, Samford gave another SEC East team a scare, leading Florida 42-28 in the first half before the Gators rallied for a 70-52 win. Samford couldn't repeat that offensive showing against Georgia.

Tight ends Darnell Washington and Brock Bowers had big gains, each leaping while making catches for 28 and 26 yards, respectively.

Georgia gave up only one first down in the first half and led 30-0 at the break. Late in the third quarter, Carson Beck replaced Bennett and Georgia's third quarterback, Brock Vandagriff, completed the game.

Samford's second possession ended with Georgia safety Dan Jackson forcing a fumble by quarterback Michael Hiers. Xavian Sorey's recovery set up the second of four field goals by Jack Podlesny.

Another defensive highlight was freshman defensive end Mykel Williams' first sack.

Samford's Michael Hiers completed 13 of 21 passes for 62 yards.

Samford coach Chris Hatcher was upbeat despite the lopsided loss.

"I thought defensively there were times we just shut them down," Hatcher said. "We get back into playing our level of competition, I expect us to come back better and faster and meaner and tougher than ever on Monday.

Stetson Bennett threw for 300 yards and two touchdowns against Samford.

Georgia running back
Kendall Milton carries for a
first down agsinst Samford.

A Defensive Force

When defending national champion Georgia lost 15 starters to the NFL draft after winning its first title since 1980 last season, the Bulldogs weren't expected to be nearly as good this year.

Georgia had five defensive starters selected in the first round of the draft, so surely it couldn't be as good on that side of the ball again.

But the Bulldogs who did come back knew their defense was in good hands with defensive tackle Jalen Carter anchoring the middle. His rise to stardom from the shadows of his former teammates is a big reason Georgia is back in the College Football Playoff for the third time in coach Kirby Smart's tenure.

"He's straight beast mode," Georgia cornerback Kelee Ringo said. "His strength is his combination of strength, speed and size. You just don't see that too often. Taking on double-teams or grabbing guys with one hand, he throws them out of his gap and goes and make plays. He's a force, and it's a great thing knowing I'm playing complementary football with his pass-rushing skills."

As No. 1 Georgia prepares to play in the College Football Playoff semifinal at the Chick-fil-A Peach Bowl in Atlanta, the Bulldogs hope Carter adds to his growing list of greatest hits, which goes back to his early days as a football and basketball player in Apopka, Florida. His impressive highlight reel at Georgia is the reason he's considered a potential No. 1 pick in the 2023 NFL draft.

For those who know Carter best, watching him sack and then pick up LSU quarterback Jayden Daniels in the SEC championship game wasn't all that surprising. They've seen him do too many amazing feats to keep count.

"Jalen is crazy," Georgia linebacker Jamon Dumas-Johnson said. "He's unblockable. He keeps doing what he's doing, he'll be top three going into the draft."

As a sophomore in 2021, Carter was coming off the bench, with three future NFL first-rounders still ahead of him. As Georgia's season transpired, however, pro scouts and opposing coaches were beginning to whisper that Carter might be better than any of them.

NFL scouts and opponents weren't the only ones suggesting Carter was the best player on Georgia's historically good defense. So were some of his teammates. Carter finished the 2021 season with 37 tackles, 33 quarterback hurries and 3 sacks. He blocked a field goal late in the third quarter against Alabama in the College Football Playoff National Championship. The Bulldogs outscored the Crimson Tide 20-9 in the fourth quarter to end their long title drought.

"He's a dominant player," said Trayvon Walker, who was the No. 1 pick in the 2022 NFL draft by the Jaguars. "He's one of those guys that can wreck the whole game, the whole interior. He's a hard worker, and if he puts his mind to do something, I feel bad [for] whoever's in his way."

Walker suggested Carter's best work has come during Georgia's practices, after an offensive lineman has challenged him.

"I can just remember times when, like say for instance, somebody just pissed Jalen off during the middle of practice," Walker said. "And, I mean, it got ugly fast. [If] somebody might say the wrong thing to him, he'll just go probably bull rush him or just hit him with a quick move. Make it a little easy. Effortless."

Devonte Wyatt, who was the 28th pick of the draft by the Packers, compares Carter to Titans Pro Bowl defensive tackle Jeffery Simmons.

"He's like a freak of nature," Wyatt said. "He's younger than me, but I was always learning stuff from him while I was in college. He's got the attitude, the effort and he loves the game. He always wants to win. When I compare him to somebody, it's someone like Jeffery Simmons — someone that's strong and can almost move guys without effort."

Bulldogs defensive lineman Jalen Carter runs during the season-opening win over Oregon in Atlanta.

Same Song, Third Verse

Once Again, Bennett and the Dawgs' D Prove Too Tough to Handle as Georgia Rolls Past Gamecocks.

September 17, 2022

COLUMBIA, S.C. — Georgia coach Kirby Smart and his No. 1 Bulldogs are sending messages to anyone who thought they were going to drop off after a national championship.

The latest statement came Saturday in a 48-7 victory over South Carolina (1-2, 0-2) in their Southeastern Conference opener, where the Gamecocks needed a touchdown with 53 seconds to go to avoid becoming the fifth shutout victim of the Bulldogs (3-0) in their past 14 games.

Meanwhile, the Georgia offense gained 547 yards, scoring on eight of its first nine possessions and was averaging nearly 10 yards a play before the backups came in and took their foot off the gas in the fourth quarter.

Even though 15 players left for the NFL after winning Georgia's first national title since 1980, there still is still plenty of talent and an attitude that winning a championship leaves behind, coach Kirby Smart said.

"That was a very special group. That's going to linger in our building," Kirby said. "Not the championship, but the way they practiced, the way they carried themselves."

Stetson Bennett went 16 for 23 for 284 yards and two touchdowns and ran for another score. Just like the Bulldogs' 49-3 victory over Oregon and 33-0 win over Samford, Bennett didn't take a snap in the fourth quarter. He reminded his teammates that it won't stay this easy.

"We're going to have to play a four-quarter game at some point. We're going to have to stay in shape," Bennett said. "This isn't going to happen every week."

Tight end Brock Bowers had five catches for 121 yards and two touchdowns and also ran for a score. Georgia let 10 players carry the ball, rushing for 212 yards.

The Bulldogs' defensive line overwhelmed South Carolina's front. A defender was in quarterback Spencer Rattler's face almost every time he dropped back more than three steps. The Oklahoma transfer got off just three deep balls, with two of them intercepted. He didn't play in the fourth quarter and was 13 of 25 for 118 yards.

"I obviously did a horse-crap job of getting our team ready to play today regardless of how many guys we had out," said South Carolina coach Shane Beamer, who was missing six defensive players. "I don't even want to hear it. We had a good enough team to go out there and compete."

The 41-point victory was Georgia's biggest against the Gamecocks in their 75 meetings. It was South Carolina's worst loss since a 56-6 defeat to Florida in 2008.

That touchdown that ruined the shutout still stung, especially after Trezman Martin intercepted a fourth quarter-pass at the Georgia 9 that appeared to snuff out the Gamecocks' last chance with 4:33 to go.

Linebacker Nolan Smith said there is no garbage time for the Georgia defense, which allowed an offensive touchdown for the first time in the last five regular-season games.

"If you are on the field, you are a starter," Smith said. "That's our body of work. That's our entire defense."

Bulldogs running back Kendall Milton makes a move upfield against South Carolina in September.

Georgia quarterback Stetson Bennett is pushed out at the one-yard line by South Carolina linebacker Brad Johnson during the first half.

Bulldogs tight end
Brock Bowers catches a
touchdown pass against
South Carolina in a 48-7
win.

Lackluster, Unbeaten

Georgia Falls Shy of a Top-Ranked Performance in Win Over Kent State.

September 24, 2022

ATHENS — Georgia hardly looked like the nation's best team, struggling to put away Kent State.

The No. 1 Bulldogs ultimately prevailed, holding on for a 39-22 victory Saturday, but their two-week run atop the rankings could be in jeopardy.

Brock Bowers scored two more touchdowns and Georgia survived a sloppy performance and surprisingly gritty effort from the Golden Flashes.

The Bulldogs (4-0) turned it over three times, struggled in the red zone, were burned on a fake punt and gave up several big plays to Kent State (1-3) in what was easily their worst performance of the season.

Was it bad enough to knock Georgia out of the top spot in the rankings? Check back Sunday.

"We don't care too much about the rankings," defensive lineman Nazir Stackhouse said. "We focus on us. It's always a 'we' thing. We're always focused on our development as a team, no matter where we are in the rankings."

Kent State had a chance to make it a one-score game with less than 13 minutes remaining after Marquez Cooper powered in from the 1 to cap a 12-play, 75-yard drive. But a two-point conversion failed, leaving the Bulldogs with a 32-22 lead.

Georgia then finished off the Golden Flashes, driving 75 yards for Kendall Milton's 1-yard plunge on fourth-and-goal with 5 1/2 minutes to go.

Georgia coach Kirby Smart insisted that he wasn't all that displeased with his team's performance.

He pointed out that the Bulldogs never had to punt, blocked a punt for a safety and finished with a 529-281 edge in total yards.

But Georgia has plenty to clean up.

"The fake punt is like a turnover," Smart said. "When you have four turnovers, you're gonna have a game like that."

Fortunately for the Bulldogs, they have Bowers.

Coming off a three-touchdown performance against South Carolina, he took it to the end zone on the second play of the game with a dazzling 75-yard run.

Going in motion to take a handoff, the sophomore tight end found a big hole around right end and never stopped running, turning on his impressive speed down the sideline in front of the Georgia bench.

Bowers also scored on a 2-yard scamper, making it three touchdowns on three carries this season for the sophomore tight end.

Or maybe he should be listed as a running back.

"I guess I'm a tight end," Bowers said. "But I just line up wherever the tell me."

Bowers strengthened his credentials as one of the nation's most dynamic offensive players.

"What a weapon he is," Smart said. "He can line up and play just about anywhere."

But Bowers was the exception for the Bulldogs on this day.

Georgia linebacker Jamon Dumas-Johnson celebrates during a win over Kent State in Athens.

Bulldogs defensive linemen Nazir Stackhouse leads a charge to tackle Kent State running back Marquez Cooper.

The Architect

Kirby Smart landed his first coaching job because the price was right.

Simple as that.

"We had only $8,000 to pay a guy," remembered Chris Hatcher, the coach who gave Smart his break at Division II Valdosta State more than two decades ago. "We were the perfect match for a guy that had no coaching experience."

From those humble beginnings — overseeing the defensive backs at a small school near the Georgia-Florida line on a poverty-level salary — Smart has evolved into one of college football's most dominant forces, the $10 million-a-year architect of a budding dynasty.

On Monday night, Smart's Georgia Bulldogs will try to become the first team in a decade to win back-to-back national titles when they take on upstart TCU in the championship game in suburban Los Angeles.

That the Bulldogs, with a 14-0 record and the Southeastern Conference crown, now have a shot at joining an elite group of repeat champions is really not at all that surprising in the current context of the program.

But when you consider what Smart has done since taking over at his alma mater from Mark Richt in 2016, the journey takes on a far more impressive luster.

The Bulldogs were a very good program under Richt.

Smart made them great.

That's just what former athletic director Greg McGarity had in mind when he hired the guy who was Nick Saban's defensive coordinator at Alabama but had never been a head coach.

During the interview process, Smart's vision of where he wanted to take Georgia was extremely specific, from the staff he wanted to hire to a detailed accounting of the financial commitment needed to take Georgia to the next level.

Still, there were many who questioned whether the Bulldogs were making the right move. For every Kirby Smart, there are a dozen Scott Frosts — those seemingly perfect coaching hires that don't work out.

"Look, every hire is a gamble," McGarity, who retired from Georgia in 2020 and now runs the Gator Bowl, said. "I don't think there's ever been any AD or president who doesn't think their hire is gonna be successful … but we all know it doesn't always work out that way."

Smart, of course, worked out just fine. Since struggling a bit in his first season, Georgia has posted a record of 72-10, lost only five regular-season SEC games, and — most impressively — supplanted Alabama as the nation's most dominant program.

Smart was a hard-nosed safety at Georgia in the late 1990s, and his immediate dream was to play in the NFL. But, after failing to hear his name called in the NFL draft and getting cut by the Indianapolis Colts, it was only natural that coaching would be his next step.

His father was a high school coach, and young Kirby had been paying close attention all along the way.

After getting his man for $8,000 — and, really, there was no one else willing to take the job — Hatcher quickly recognized what a bargain it was.

"Once I got to know him and watch him coach, I realized that — first of all, he's extremely smart and he's a tremendous worker," said Hatcher, now the coach at Alabama's Samford University. "And he brought to the team —— what's the right word for it? — yeah, he's a very intense guy, but it was more of a competitive spirit that he had about him."

Smart moved on after two highly successful seasons at Valdosta State, got his graduate degree from Florida State and then began the most significant working relationship of his career.

Georgia coach Kirby Smart watches from the sidelines during the Peach Bowl against Ohio State.

Saban, who was then the head coach at LSU, hired Smart as his defensive backs coach in 2004. He would be Smart's boss and mentor for 10 of the next 11 seasons, the only interruption being a single season as Richt's running backs coach.

In 2008, after an ill-fated stint in the NFL and a rebuilding year at Alabama, Saban was ready to unleash perhaps the greatest dynasty in the history of college football. Smart was his defensive coordinator and right-hand man as the Crimson Tide ripped off four national titles in an eight-year span, gleaning many of the lessons that would serve him so well running his own program.

"He learned from probably the greatest of all time," Georgia quarterback Stetson Bennett said. "He learned and he took notes … and then he made it his."

Bennett has been along for most of the ride. He arrived at Georgia as a walk-in 2017, which was Smart's breakout year after going a middling 8-5 in his debut season. The Bulldogs won their first SEC title in a dozen years and reached the College Football Playoff title game, where they lost to Saban and the Tide in an overtime thriller.

Even in defeat, it was already clear that Smart was far more than just Saban Lite.

"He is a big believer in discipline and schedule and all that stuff. And that's good and fine, but he's also brilliant. He learns," Bennett said. "And everything at the end of the day is about the University of Georgia winning. That goes from our facilities, goes to recruiting, raising money, practice, recovery, nutrition, mental health, everything."

Georgia quarterback Stetson Bennett and coach Kirby Smart celebrate after defeating LSU in the SEC Championshp game on December 3 in Atlanta.

First Real Test Passed

Bulldogs Rally from Double-Digit Deficit, Remain Unbeaten Despite Missouri's Best Effort.

October 1, 2022

COLUMBIA, Mo. — The two most important characteristics that Georgia coach Kirby Smart seeks in his team are composure and resiliency, and the top-ranked Bulldogs needed to rely on both to rally past Missouri on Saturday night.

Or, as Smart put it: "We had to OD on those."

Kept out of the end zone until the fourth quarter and facing a 10-point deficit, the Bulldogs got their run game going just in time to avoid the upset. Kendall Milton finished off one long drive with a touchdown, then Daijun Edwards got into the end zone with just over four minutes to go, lifting the Bulldogs to a 26-22 victory.

"They played really physical and really hard and whipped us up front, but I'm really proud of us," Smart said. "We always talk about rising to the competitive nature of the opportunity and we did that tonight."

The Bulldogs (5-0, 2-0 SEC) trailed almost the entire way before finally solving the red-zone woes that forced Jack Podlesny into kicking four field goals. Quarterback Stetson Bennett also struggled all night against the blitzing Missouri defense, but the leader of the defending national champions still wound up with 312 yards passing and no interceptions.

"It felt like an SEC game in the fourth quarter that we had to win," Bennett said afterward. "They have pride too. They expect to win too. And they played hard, too."

Brady Cook had 192 yards passing and a touchdown for the Tigers (2-3, 0-2), who have never beaten a top-ranked team in 17 tries.

"We were self-inflicted wounds away from winning that game," Tigers coach Eli Drinkwitz said.

The Tigers carried their angst right into the game. Their rebuilt defense behind coordinator Blake Baker forced an early fumble and bunch of punts, and Missouri capitalized on the good field position. Mevis made the first of his field goals to put the Bulldogs in their first hole of the season.

They wound up spending the rest of the night digging out of it.

Taking advantage of breakdowns by Georgia's top-ranked scoring defense, Cook found Dominic Lovett for a 36-yard gain, then got 6-foot-6 tight end Tyler Stephens to make a slick one-handed grab for a walk-in touchdown and 10-0 lead.

After another fumble by the Bulldogs, Mevis added a 49-yarder to extend the Tigers' advantage.

"We knew we were going to get everything they had," Georgia center Sedrick Van Pran said.

The Bulldogs finally got on the score board on Podlesny's 40-yard field goal, only to watch Division II transfer Cody Schrader rip off a 63-yard run on the Tigers' next possession. He was finally tackled at the goal line, and the Bulldogs made a much-needed stand, but Mevis nevertheless added a chip-shot field goal to restore the 16-3 lead.

Even when the Bulldogs successfully faked a field goal late in the first half only to settle for one anyway, then had to kick another after a 16-play drive that took up half the third quarter.

Georgia wide receiver Dominick Blaylock makes a catch as Missouri defensive back Ennis Rakestraw Jr. has close coverage in the second quarter.

Bulldogs linebacker Nolan Smith chases down Tigers quarterback Brady Cook for a sack.

Dawgs Roll Past Tigers

Georgia Turns Deep South's Oldest Rivalry into Laugher.

October 8, 2022

ATHENS — Georgia gets held to an almost impossible standard these days. That goes with being the defending national champions.

"I think we just got to play football," quarterback Stetson Bennett said. "I mean, it's just football. It's X's and O's. It's have fun with your brother and go jump on him."

The Bulldogs had plenty to enjoy Saturday in a 42-10 victory against rival Auburn that started a little sluggish, but turned into a laugher.

Bennett sprinted 64 yards for a touchdown, Daijun Edwards scored three times on the ground and No. 2 Georgia ran over the listless Tigers.

"I think we're getting just like, 'Ah, well, you know it wasn't perfect, so I'm going to be miserable.' Like, no. We played a good game. We got a lot of things to get better at. We just get better at them next week," Bennett said. "But we're going to enjoy this week."

Bennett's career-long run on the first play of the fourth quarter was the biggest of the day for a Bulldogs offense that mostly plodded along for the first three.

The Bulldogs (6-0, 3-0 Southeastern Conference) got two short touchdown runs by Edwards and one from Kenny McIntosh to build a 21-3 in the third quarter.

Then Bennett found a huge swath of empty green grass on a quarterback draw and managed to beat a chasing pack of Tigers to the goal line to make it 28-3.

"Usually, I'm pretty smart about getting down because I know I'm not the biggest guy. But there was nobody there. And I was like, alright, well, we're just gonna keep rolling," Bennett said.

Georgia ran its winning streak to six in the series, has not lost the Deep South's Oldest Rivalry at home since 2005 and leads overall 63-56.

Getting little help from its offense, Auburn's defense seemed to wear down and gave up 292 yards and six touchdowns rushing.

Robby Ashford was 13 for 38 for 168 yards while frequently scrambling to elude pressure for the Tigers (3-3, 1-2).

Coming off consecutive lackluster performances, the Bulldogs were once again spotty offensively in the first half.

Georgia opened up a 14-0 lead in the second quarter, turning two short-field possessions into touchdowns.

First, a failed Auburn faked punt in Georgia territory set up the Bulldogs at the Tigers' 36. McIntosh finished with a 1-yard TD run.

Ladd McConkey's 38-yard punt return put Georgia at the Auburn 31 and Edwards scored from a yard out to put the Bulldogs up two scores.

And that was pretty much all they needed against an Auburn team that has not scored more than 17 points in any of its last four games under beleaguered second-year coach Bryan Harsin, who said he was mostly pleased with his defense.

Georgia wide receiver Ladd McConkey returns a punt during a 42-10 rout of Auburn.

"At some point you got to put some points on the board. You got to even the game out. You got to keep it close. You got to give your guys hope," he said.

Georgia running back
Daijun Edwards (30)
celebrates a touchdown
against Auburn with Marcus
Rosemy-Jacksaint.

Georgia mascot UGA X rests in his sideline dawghouse during the win over Auburn in October.

UGA X

Back Home at the Top

Georgia
Blows Out
Vanderbilt,
Solidifies
Number
One Spot in
Polls.

October 15, 2022

ATHENS — Stetson Bennett grimaced when told the news.

The Atlanta Braves were knocked out of the Major League Baseball playoffs Saturday.

After No. 1 Georgia romped to a 55-0 victory over Vanderbilt, the Bulldogs' veteran quarterback pointed to his favorite baseball team — the reigning World Series champions — as an example of how fleeting a title can be.

"Are we gonna cash our chips in after so-and-so games, or are we gonna keep going, keep going, and know this isn't over until its over?" asked Bennett, whose team is seeking its second straight national championship.

Unlike the Braves, the Bulldogs are still on track.

Bennett threw for 289 yards and two touchdowns — his first scoring passes in nearly a month — and Georgia stamped its return to the No. 1 ranking with a blowout of the lowly Commodores.

Georgia (7-0, 4-0 Southeastern Conference) led 28-0 at halftime and shook off three straight weeks of rather lackluster performances.

Those games provided a valuable lesson in what it takes to repeat as a champion.

"It's tough," Bennett said. "We are not King Kong standing atop the Empire State Building. We've gotta work and execute each week, go out there and expect a dog fight until it's not one."

Bennett was nearly perfect in the first half, completing 18 of 20 for 211 yards. Darnell Washington, the 6-foot-7 tight end who usually plays a supporting role to Brock Bowers, came up big with four catches for 78 yards, including a one-handed dazzler.

"It's like throwing to the Pacific Ocean," Bennett quipped.

Bennett hooked up with Kenny McIntosh on an 11-yard scoring play — the quarterback's first TD pass in four weeks — and followed with a 10-yard scoring toss to Dominick Blaylock.

"It was good to get in the end zone," Bennett said. "But it was better to score 55."

McIntosh added a 7-yard scoring run, while Daijun Edwards powered in from the 1 to spark a second-half exodus of red-clad Georgia fans looking to beat the traffic.

Carson Beck took over for Bennett in the final quarter, throwing two more touchdown passes that merely added to Vandy's pain.

The Commodores (3-4, 0-3) dropped their 24th straight game in the SEC. They last won a conference game on Oct 19, 2019, beating Missouri 21-14.

At the halftime break, Georgia held a commanding 296-72 edge in total yards and 16-4 advantage in first downs.

"A very frustrating afternoon," coach Clark Lea said. "We were never able to get a drive going. For us, it's been this way all year It's just where we are. It's a recipe for disaster."

The Bulldogs defense posted its second shutout of the season, limiting Vandy to just 45 yards rushing and 150 overall.

Georgia piled up 579 total yards.

Georgia defensive lineman Mykel Williams applies pressure during a 55-0 win over Vanderbilt.

Georgia receiver Jackson Meeks has his jersey grabbed by Vanderbilt linebacker CJ Taylor as Vanderbilt cornerback Tyson Russell (8) makes a tackle in the second half.

Cocktail Party Cruise

Georgia
Pulls Away
from Florida
Late, Sets up
Showdown
with Vols.

October 29, 2022

JACKSONVILLE, Fla. — Top-ranked Georgia expects to eventually benefit from a game like this. It might happen next year. Or maybe next week.

Daijun Edwards and Kenny McIntosh ran for two touchdowns each, and the Bulldogs pulled away from Florida following a second-half scare to win 42-20 Saturday night in the rivalry dubbed "the World's Largest Outdoor Cocktail Party."

Next up: No. 3 Tennessee, a game that could have Southeastern Conference and College Football Playoff implications. Georgia might not have the same margin for error against the Volunteers as it enjoyed against Florida.

The defending national champion Bulldogs (8-0, 5-0 SEC) looked to be in trouble when the Gators (4-4, 1-4) scored the first 17 points of the third quarter and turned a 28-3 deficit into a one-score game.

But the Dawgs answered in resounding fashion with consecutive touchdown drives to seal their 10th consecutive victory. It was Georgia's fifth win over Florida in the last six seasons.

"I don't enjoy losing the momentum in the game," Dawgs coach Kirby Smart said. "I enjoy the fact that we never blinked. ... There's two things (that happen) when adversity hits: you fracture or you connect. Our team connected."

This one was dedicated to legendary Georgia coach Vince Dooley, who died Friday at age 90.

Dooley dominated the Georgia-Florida series during his coaching career, going 17-7-1 against the Gators. The most famous victory came in 1980, when Lindsay Scott hauled in a 93-yard touchdown pass from Buck Belue in the closing minute. The improbable 26-21 triumph propelled Georgia to a perfect season and their first consensus national title.

"Such an ambassador for our program and all of college football," Smart said. "I know if he was looking down on that one, he would have enjoyed the first half. I don't know that he would have enjoyed the second one."

Florida had all the momentum in the third quarter after Amari Burney forced two turnovers following Trevor Etienne's TD run. Burney stripped McIntosh and intercepted a pass from Stetson Bennett.

"They didn't stop us other than that," Bennett said. "We answered really well after the pick I threw and went right down the field. Everybody answered the call whenever they were asked."

Georgia put the game away thanks to a few key fourth downs. Bennett connected with tight end Brock Bowers on a fourth-and-7 play to set up one touchdown in-between Florida's two failed attempts to move the chains on fourth down.

"Yeah, it's a turnover on downs and turnovers affect the outcome of the game," Florida coach Billy Napier said. "No different than them turning the ball over allowed them to get us back in the game. ... We had our opportunities. We can coach better. We can play better."

Georgia played nearly flawless football down the stretch and finished with 555 yards against Florida's beleaguered defense. Edwards had 106 yards rushing, including a 22-yard TD run that halted Florida's comeback. McIntosh added 90 on the ground.

Georgia quarterback Stetson Bennett is lifted in the air by offensive lineman Warren McClendon during a 42-20 win over Florida.

Bulldogs defensive lineman Jalen Carter tries to wrap up Florida quarterback Anthony Richardson.

Georgia running back Daijun Edwards (30) runs for a 22-yard touchdown past Florida cornerback Avery Helm (24) and defensive lineman Princely Umanmielen.

Georgia tight end Brock Bowers catches a pass against Florida.

Georgia players and coach Kirby Smart celebrate with fans after defeating Florida 42-20.

Tennessee Dispatched

Bennett
Outduels
Tennessee's
Hooker,
Bulldogs
Remain
Unbeaten.

November 5, 2022

A THENS In the biggest games, Stetson Bennett seems to rise to the occasion and above his often more heralded counterparts.

Bennett threw two touchdown passes and ran for a score as No. 1 Georgia shut down Hendon Hooker and the Vols' high-powered offense to win a Southeastern Conference showdown of the nation's top-ranked teams 27-13 Saturday.

After leading the Bulldogs to a national title last season, Bennett improved to 23-3 as a starter at Georgia.

"Competitive excellence, competitive toughness," said Georgia coach Kirby Smart when asked about Bennett's ability to shine on the grandest stages.

"He's a winner. Let's be honest. The guy knows how to win."

Bennett passed for 257 yards, completing 17 of 25 passes. He had a 13-yard scoring run in the matchup against Hooker, regarded as a Heisman Trophy favorite. Maybe Bennett should be now?

Bennett insisted his only motivation was for the team's hopes of returning to the SEC championship game, not for his personal validation "because at the end of the day we're playing for the East and if we lost it's a lower percentage we're playing in Atlanta."

Added Bennett: "I don't really care about quarterback vs. quarterback."

Georgia (9-0, 6-0 Southeastern Conference) turned the 25th regular-season matchup of the top two teams in the AP poll into a rout that made clear the defending national champions are still the team to beat.

"I kind of feel like it was a statement win," said Georgia wide receiver Ladd McConkey, who had five catches for 94 yards and a touchdown.

In a deafening and soggy Sanford Stadium, Georgia led 27-6 before Tennessee scored its first touchdown with 4:15 remaining.

Hooker, whose Heisman hopes were bolstered by a win over Alabama last month, passed for only 195 yards for Tennessee (8-1, 4-1). Hooker was sacked six times by star defensive tackle Jalen Carter and the Bulldogs.

Tennessee wide receiver Jalin Hyatt said Georgia's defense was "way more physical than Alabama."

Georgia's special teams put more pressure on Tennessee. Punter Brett Thorson nailed a 75-yarder that went out of bounds at the Tennessee 1 in the first quarter. Jack Podlesny kicked two field goals.

Hooker threw an interception, lost a fumble that nearly resulted in a safety for Georgia and didn't throw a touchdown pass.

"They are a great ball team," Hooker said. "They played extremely hard, and they got the win today. We have got to clean some things up. It is a learning process."

The Volunteers came in averaging almost 50 points per game.

The Volunteers rode that Alabama victory to the top spot in the first College Football Playoff ranking. Georgia was No. 3 in last week's CFP ranking.

That will change Tuesday.

Georgia defensive back Jaheim Singletary breaks up a pass intended for Tennessee receiver Cedric Tillman during a 27-13 win.

Georgia receiver Marcus Rosemy-Jacksaint catches a touchdown during a win over Tennessee.

Georgia quarterback
Stetson Bennett throws
from the pocket in the first
half against the Vols.

Georgia defensive lineman Tyrion Ingram-Dawkins reacts after recovering a fumble during the second half.

Georgia fans pay tribute to former head football coach Vince Dooley and former football star Charlie Trippi, who both recently died, before the game against Tennessee.

The Monken Impact

Georgia fans' ears are still ringing from the Dawgs' miracle last-second victory over Ohio State in Saturday's Peach Bowl, but it wasn't all that long ago that Georgia head coach Kirby Smart walked off that same Mercedes-Benz Stadium field looking like a relic, a dinosaur, a holdover from a bygone era.

The date was December 7, 2019; the game was the SEC championship; and the then-fourth-ranked Bulldogs couldn't even throw a scare into the Joe Burrow-led LSU Tigers. Burrow masterminded a 37-10 win over Georgia that wasn't even that close, a beatdown so complete that it both clinched Burrow's Heisman candidacy and consigned Georgia, once again, to the ranks of regular-season tough guys who wilted when the games mattered.

Comparing anyone to LSU-era Joe Burrow and any offense to the 2019 Tigers is an exercise in futility, but even so, that game showed just how far off the pace Georgia had slipped. Georgia's quarterback that season was Jake Fromm, who'd led the Bulldogs to the national championship game two years earlier but sputtered down the stretch in 2019. By the time of that SEC championship, Fromm was on a five-game run of sub-50-percent completions, and his two interceptions against LSU doomed any chance the Dawgs had of staying competitive.

The grumbling around Athens grew into growling. Something had to change, pronto. Something did, and three years later, Georgia is playing for its second straight national title.

That something: an itinerant, then-unemployed career coordinator who has unlocked Georgia's offense, turned a walk-on into a Heisman finalist, and positioned the Bulldogs as college football's next great dynasty. When Smart went looking to level up his struggling offense, he rung up Todd Monken, and that has made all the difference. Monken was coming off a one-year stint as the Browns' offensive coordinator, a tenure that ended abruptly when the Browns dismissed head coach Freddie Kitchens and the incoming Kevin Stefanski cleaned house. Cleveland was the latest in a 30-year, 11-stop career that encompassed everything from the NFL (Browns, Jags, Bucs) to college football's elite (Notre Dame, LSU) to, well … Grand Valley State. In his lone head coaching stint, he took a Southern Miss team that had gone 0-12 the year before he arrived and transformed it into a 9-5 squad within three seasons.

Monken crafts complex, multilevel offensive schemes that, at their heart, follow a simple philosophy: "You recruit good players," he said prior to the Peach Bowl. "You have a structure and a system. And then you go to work."

Of course, the structure and the system work a whole lot better when you have recruits on the level of a Georgia. Under Monken's guidance, Georgia went from being ranked 59th nationally in total offense in 2019, the year before he arrived, up to eighth this season. The Bulldogs' improvement through the air has flown on a similar trajectory, from 72nd in passing yardage in 2019 up to 15th this year … and, along the way, setting the stage for a national championship and Georgia's first Heisman finalist since running back Garrison Hearst in 1992.

"I feel like before he got here, I didn't really understand football," said Georgia QB Stetson Bennett, who finished fourth in Heisman voting. "It's weird, even in 2020, [I] didn't really know what was going on … Maybe I'm a slow learner, but finally it did start clicking whenever he would tell me the same thing for the 20th time."

"When you have talent and they play their rear ends off and they work and have attention to detail," Monken said, "the game is just a byproduct of that."

The result is an attack that draws the admiration even of the coaches tasked with stopping it. "The versatility of the offense with the multiple tight ends who are extremely talented, receivers who can make plays in various ways throughout the field, running backs who can attack you both inside and outside and a quarterback who just does a marvelous job of managing the whole thing," Ohio State defensive coordinator Jim Knowles said just days before having to face Monken's creation.

"It's a complete offense. It's developed like an NFL offense."

Georgia offensive coordinator Todd Monken watches drills during spring practice with quarterback Gunner Stockton.

Division Crown Still Fits

Bennett
Turns in
Another
Standout
Performance,
Georgia
Seals Date
in SEC Title
Game.

November 12, 2022

STARKVILLE, Miss. — No. 1 Georgia is going to the SEC championship game.

Stetson Bennett and company just keep rolling along.

Bennett threw for three touchdowns, and undefeated Georgia beat Mississippi State 45-19 on Saturday night.

"I'm really proud of our team. When you go on the road in the SEC in an environment like this at night, there's tremendous adversity and our guys responded again and again," coach Kirby Smart said. "Our guys kept responding and competing."

With the victory, the East Division champion Bulldogs secured a spot in the SEC championship. They will take on LSU in Atlanta on Dec. 3.

It was a dominating effort by the Bulldogs (10-0, 7-0, No. 1 CFP), who put up 468 yards of offense. Bennett led the way, going 25 for 37 for 289 yards with two interceptions. Georgia also rushed for 179 yards.

"It was a team win and we made plays when we needed them," Bennett said.

Mississippi State (6-4, 3-4) struggled to consistently produce against Georgia on the offensive side. Will Rogers went 29 for 51 for 263 yards and a touchdown. Mississippi State rushed for just 47 yards on 15 carries. Rufus Harvey led MSU with six catches for 66 yards and a score.

"They have all five-star players. They're pretty good on defense and coach Smart does a really good job," Rogers said. "They had a really good scheme for what we were doing and it's hard to finish drives on a good team."

Georgia turned the ball over twice on interceptions by Bennett and had another near turnover in the red zone in the first half when a fumble was nullified after the play was blown dead.

Georgia grabbed control with a big second half. Receiver Ladd McConkey had a 70-yard touchdown run and a 17-yard TD reception to help Georgia open a 31-12 lead.

Mississippi State got off to a tough start, but Zavion Thomas' 63-yard punt return trimmed Georgia's lead to 17-12 at halftime.

"I thought early on we did some good things. There was kind of a feel-out process to see what we were capable of doing," coach Mike Leach said. "I thought we left two obvious scores out there which would not be too tough to have. We did more good things than bad, but I thought that we could have finished drives better."

Georgia tight end Brock Bowers runs after a catch against Mississippi State during a 45-19 victory.

Georgia defensive lineman Nazir Stackhouse celebrates after the Bulldogs defeated Mississippi State.

Bulldogs lineback Smael Mondon pulls the jersey of Mississippi State receiver Austin Williams while making a tackle.

Perfect Again

Defense Stands Tall as Georgia Finishes Another SEC Season Unbeaten, and Barely Tested.

November 19, 2022

LEXINGTON, Ky. — Between Kenny McIntosh and Jack Podlesny, top-ranked Georgia got all the important points it needed on a day where style points weren't possible.

McIntosh rushed for a career-best 143 yards, including a crucial 9-yard score late in the third quarter, and the Bulldogs withstood Kentucky's fourth-quarter rally Saturday for a 16-6 win and its second consecutive unbeaten season in the Southeastern Conference.

The Bulldogs (11-0, 8-0 SEC, No. 1 CFP) clinched the Eastern Division title last week and sought another perfect finish in league play. They came away as just the third SEC team since 1992 to post consecutive 8-0 league marks, following Alabama (2008-09) and Florida (1995-96).

Georgia's success wasn't easy in cold, windy conditions, and it settled for three Podlesny field goals before McIntosh's TD provided a needed cushion.

"With these weather conditions, we're going to play these kind of games like this," coach Kirby Smart said. "But I'm really proud of when our guys' backs are against the wall, how they come out fighting with what they do.

"Certainly, we could've played better, probably in the red area. They could have stopped some drives defensively; we gave them a couple of conversions on penalties. I have to give Kentucky a lot of credit for bouncing back and being a really physical football team."

Georgia's chance to pad the lead ended on downs at Kentucky's 1. The Wildcats to made it interesting with a 99-yard drive that ended with Will Levis' 8-yard touchdown pass to Barion Brown. Levis' two-point conversion pass failed, and the chance to make it a one-score game died when Matt Ruffalo's field goal hooked left after a low, rolling snap.

Kentucky (6-5, 3-5) then turned it over on downs and lost for the fifth time in seven games.

McIntosh rushed a career-high 19 times with a 26-yarder for the Bulldogs, who outgained Kentucky 365-297 and 247-89 on the ground.

"It was real big," McIntosh said of his TD. "We had been driving the ball the whole field, but we knew that we needed to score on that drive to come out strong and get the ball rolling on the ground. We had preached during halftime that we needed to go out there and start stronger and be physical on the line of scrimmage."

The senior back's previous best was 90 yards on 16 attempts against Florida last month.

"Kenny ran the ball really well tonight," Smart added. "Probably could've had more, but he had to share with some other guys."

Georgia quarterback Stetson Bennett completed 13 of 19 for 116 yards with an interception.

Levis completed 20 of 31 for 206 yards with an interception for Kentucky.

The Wildcats had been picked to finish second behind Georgia in the East and were ranked as high as No. 7 in the AP Top 25 in late September before spiraling downward with painful division losses to South Carolina, No. 5 Tennessee and last week's shocking 24-21 home loss to Vanderbilt that snapped the Commodores' 26-game SEC losing streak.

Georgia linebacker Smael Mondon Jr. (2) tackles Kentucky running back Chris Rodriguez Jr. during a 16-6 win to end the SEC season for the Bulldogs.

Kentucky defenders bring down Georgia running back Kenny McIntosh at the end of a run.

Georgia's Kelee Ringo makes a clutch interception against Kentucky during a 16-6 win.

Georgia placekicker Jack Podlesny connects on one of his three field goals against the Wildcats.

Slow Start? No Problem

Bulldogs
Finish
Regular
Season
Unbeaten
Behind
Bruising
Rushing
Attack.

November 26, 2022

ATHENS — A perfect regular season isn't good enough for Stetson Bennett and No. 1 Georgia.

Bennett threw two touchdown passes and Georgia completed back-to-back undefeated regular seasons for the first time in school history by overcoming a slow start to beat Georgia Tech 37-14 on Saturday.

"It is special," said Bennett of the undefeated regular season, "but we didn't enter this season trying to go 12-0. We want to go 15-0."

Georgia (No. 1 CFP) was down 7-0 early and led only 10-7 at halftime. Then the Bulldogs overpowered the Yellow Jackets (5-7) with their running game to score 37 unanswered points and notch their fifth consecutive win in the state rivalry.

The defending national champion Bulldogs are in good position to retain their top College Football Playoff ranking entering next week's Southeastern Conference championship game against No. 6 LSU.

Kenny McIntosh and Kendall Milton ran for touchdowns. Georgia outrushed Georgia Tech 264-40.

"Every drive we ran the ball, the running backs stepped up and answered the bell," McIntosh said.

The slow start was frustrating for Bennett, but the senior couldn't complain about the finish in his final home game.

"I really wasn't happy with the way we started today but we still scored 37," Bennett said. "... We ran the ball really well today."

Mistakes in the third quarter hurt the Yellow Jackets' chance at spoiling the Bulldogs' history-making day. Following a low snap, punter David Shanahan was tackled at the Georgia Tech 17. That set up Bennett's second scoring pass, a 1-yarder to tight end Brock Bowers on a fourth-down play.

Georgia Tech freshman running back Jamie Felix's fumble was recovered by Georgia's Robert Beal on the Yellow Jackets' next play, setting up a 36-yard field goal by Jack Podlesny.

"We made some mistakes in the second half and couldn't sustain some drives," Georgia Tech interim coach Brent Key said. "... We can't have those in big games like that, especially when you know going into it that it's going to be a field possession game and they have an explosive offense."

Georgia pulled away in the fourth quarter. Bennett's 83-yard pass to McIntosh — the Bulldogs' longest pass of the season — set up McIntosh's 2-yard scoring run. Milton added a 44-yard scoring run.

Georgia Tech became the first team to score a first-quarter touchdown against Georgia this season. Zach Gibson completed a 34-yard pass to Nate McCollum on a fourth and 9 play to the Georgia 7.

Backup quarterback Taisun Phommachanh's 7-yard scoring run capped the touchdown drive.

Georgia quarterback Stetson Bennett sets up to throw during the first half against Georgia Tech.

Georgia Tech running back Dontae Smith is stopped by Georgia defenders Robert Beal Jr. (33) and Mykel Williams (13) during the first half.

Georgia coach Kirby Smart and his players hoist the Governor's Cup after defeating Georgia Tech.

A Georgia Legend

Stetson Bennett wouldn't allow himself to bask so long in the celebration following last season's national championship that it would be more difficult to make a run at a repeat title this year.

Bennett, who began his career at Georgia as a walk-on, has had many critics and coaches — even on his own team — tell him what he can't do. He refused to be distracted by the praise that came with his lead role on the Bulldogs' first national championship since 1980 last season.

Now Bennett has No. 1 Georgia one win away from the school's first back-to-back titles.

No team has won consecutive championships in the first eight years of the CFP. Alabama quarterback A.J. McCarron won back-to-back BCS national championships in the 2011 and 2012 seasons. Before that, the last quarterback to win two straight titles was Nebraska's Tommie Frazier in 1994-95.

Bennett said he understands why back-to-back titles are so rare.

"Yeah man, these pats on the back feel good, you know?" Bennett said. "And then you start to believe what they've told you, and it's never true. Good or bad, it's never true. And then you literally forget how you did it and it's the craziest thing in the world. Because you want to but you took so much time off that you've forgotten how to do the work."

Bennett, all of 5-feet-11 and 190 pounds, knew he couldn't afford to stop working. There are too many four- and five-star quarterbacks waiting for an opportunity — on the Georgia depth chart or in the transfer portal.

Bennett met with Georgia coach Kirby Smart shortly after the national title win and asked the coach pointed questions. At some point before spring practice, everyone seemed clear that Bennett was Georgia's best option at quarterback even though three players beneath him on the depth chart were each ranked No. 17 (Brock Vandagriff, Class of 2021), No. 124 (Gunner Stockton, Class of 2022) and No. 250 (Carson Beck, Class of 2020) in the nation by 247Sports as high schoolers. (Bennett was ranked No. 2,569 in the Class of 2017)

"I was not a big, prized recruit or anything like that and I didn't look like one and there was really no threat of me becoming one, if we're being frank," Bennett said.

Bennett walked on at Georgia in 2017, transferred to Jones College in Ellisville, Mississippi, in 2018 and then returned to Georgia more determined than ever, even if it meant working on the scout team.

He now is 27-3 as a starter and has consistently flourished in Georgia's biggest games, disproving his label as a game manager on a run-first offense.

Bennett threw a combined nine touchdown passes with no interceptions in last season's CFP wins over Michigan and Alabama and in a 50-30 win over LSU in the Southeastern Conference championship game on Dec. 3. He was named offensive MVP in all three games.

Georgia center Sedrick Van Pran says Bennett's success on the game's biggest stages is easy to understand.

"I think it's the same thing that I see every game," Van Pran said. "It's just his preparation. ... He's a guy who just works really hard. I think that may come from him being an underdog and things like that."

Bennett completed 23 of 29 passes for 274 yards and four touchdowns in the win over LSU.

"Obviously he has shown up big," said Georgia tight end Brock Bowers. "That comes through all the preparation that we do. His personality just shows up in these bigger games and being able to perform on the biggest stages."

Bennett has tied Eric Zeier's school record with 269 completions this season while passing for 3,425 yards and 20 touchdowns. Bennett said he has shored up his mechanics in the last year, and is better at self-correcting when his delivery gets out of sorts. Most of his improvement, though, is on the mental side of the game, better understanding what each play is trying to accomplish.

Bulldogs quarterback Stetson Bennett throws during pregame warm-ups before the Peach Bowl against Ohio State on December 31.

No Signs of Stopping

Bulldogs Lay Claim to First SEC Title Since 2017, Seal Top Spot in College Football Playoff.

December 3, 2022

ATLANTA — Georgia swatted away the field goal attempt, the ball spinning to a stop at its 4-yard line. The LSU players trudged off the field, thinking the play was over.

Christopher Smith knew better. He suddenly scooped it up and took off the other way, sprinting 96 yards for a touchdown that epitomized the Bulldogs program.

They were a step ahead of LSU on Saturday.

They've been a step ahead of everyone for two years now.

With all sorts of turmoil behind them in the rankings, Georgia headed to the College Football Playoff as the clear No. 1, dismantling the No. 11 Tigers 50-30 in the Southeastern Conference championship game Saturday.

Stetson Bennett's threw a season-high four touchdown passes in another stellar postseason performance, while Smith's heads-up play gave the Bulldogs an early spark.

"I've got good players around me. I'm not that bad at football, either," Bennett said with a smile. "We've got a good team."

Georgia (13-0, No. 1 CFP) also caught a big break when Smith deflected a pass that bounced off an LSU receiver's helmet and wound up being picked off by the Bulldogs, setting up a score that contributed to a 35-10 lead by halftime.

LSU quarterback Jayden Daniels re-injured a sore right ankle late in the second quarter, giving way to Garrett Nussmeier in the second half.

The backup guiding the Tigers (9-4, No. 14 CFP) to three touchdowns, but it wasn't nearly enough.

Georgia accomplished something that not even last season's national championship squad could do — win its first SEC title since 2017. The Bulldogs were denied in this game a year ago by Alabama, before bouncing back to beat the Crimson Tide in the title game.

"I don't want one kid to walk out of our program without an SEC championship ring in their careers," coach Kirby Smart said. "That could've happened. They said enough is enough and got 'em one tonight."

Georgia heads into the playoff assured of a return trip to Atlanta for a de facto semifinal home game at Mercedes-Benz Stadium, just 75 miles from its Athens campus.

LSU's outside hopes of crashing the four-team playoff field were wiped out a week ago by a stunning loss at Texas A&M, one of several upsets that will give the selection committee plenty to think about before its announcement Sunday.

Tennessee and Clemson also ruined their playoff hopes with losses late in the regular season, while No. 4 Southern California is presumably out after getting blown out by Utah in the Pac-12 title game Friday night.

Just as the SEC game was kicking off, No. 3 TCU lost to Kansas State in overtime for the Big 12 championship, further clouding a playoff picture that suddenly looks much more favorable for No. 5 Ohio State and No. 6 Alabama.

No matter who makes the elite field, Georgia is firmly focused on becoming the first repeat national champion since Alabama in 2011-12, having won all but one game this

Stetson Bennett lifts up the MVP trophy after a 50-30 win over LSU in the SEC Championship Game.

season by double-digit margins.

"I've tried not to play attention to any of it," Smart said of all the chaos. "It didn't matter to me. That's so far away."

The Bulldogs showed they are more than just a bunch of talented athletes — this is a smart, well-coached group.

When Nazir Stackhouse burst through the middle of the line to block LSU's 32-yard field goal attempt late in the first quarter, Smith knew what to do.

"That's a scenario we go over a lot in practice," he said.

He looked toward the sideline to see if it was OK to grab it.

"You're not allowed to pick it up unless you can score with it," Smart said.

Smith took care of the rest, dashing to the end zone without a Tigers player in sight.

LSU coach Brian Kelly blamed himself and his staff for allowing the play to happen.

"Obviously, we did a poor job if coaching," he said. "It's our responsibility to have our guys alert in that situation. They were not alert."

LSU quickly tied it up on Daniels' 53-yard touchdown pass to Kayshon Boutte, only to have Bennett take control from there.

The sixth-year senior, a former walk-on who was offensive MVP of both Georgia playoff wins a year ago, struck for four TD passes in a less than 15-minute span: 3 yards to Brock Bowers, 22 yards to Ladd McConkey, 14 yards to Darnell Washington and 3 yards to Dillon Bell.

Just like that, Georgia led 35-7.

"I was in a zone," Bennett said.

It's been that way for two years now.

Georgia defensive back Malaki Starks reacts as teammate Christopher Smith returns a blocked LSU field goal attempt for a touchdown in the first half.

Georgia defensive lineman Warren Brinson recovers a fumble by LSU quarterback Garrett Nussmeier during the second half.

Georgia running back Kenny McIntosh crosses the goal line against LSU in the SEC Championship.

Kirby Smart and the Georgia players celebrate on the field after winning the SEC title.

Ringing In The Cheers

Legend of Bennett Grows, Bulldogs Advance to Title Game When Last-Second Kick Falls Short at Stroke of Midnight on New Year's Eve.

December 31, 2022

ATLANTA — The legend of Georgia quarterback Stetson Bennett would have endured for generations even if the confetti of last season's celebration served as the backdrop in the story's final scene. The former walk-on led the Bulldogs to a national title a year ago, and that lasts forever. But Bennett decided to return for his sixth season of college football, so here he is now, poised on the sport's biggest stage, throwing the winning touchdown in the final minute of a semifinal matchup against Ohio State.

Bennett's 10-yard pass to Adonai Mitchell lifted top-seeded Georgia ahead with 54 seconds to go. The Buckeyes then drove down the field in search of a game-winning field goal attempt, but Noah Ruggles's 50-yard kick was wide left, sealing the Bulldogs' 42-41 Peach Bowl win on Saturday night. After the miss, Georgia's celebration could begin. Bennett raced onto the field with his arms outstretched, overcome with joy.

Chasing a second consecutive national title, Bennett authored the ferocious rally for the Bulldogs, who entered the fourth quarter of this College Football Playoff matchup with their title hopes fading. Georgia scored 18 points in the final period, and its defense held firm. The Bulldogs kept Ohio State quarterback C.J. Stroud from becoming the game's headliner with late heroics and instead forced the long field goal that missed.

Stroud, a Heisman Trophy finalist like Bennett, had a brilliant performance against Georgia's vaunted defense. But Bennett had the final say, throwing for 398 yards and three touchdowns, none more important than the one he spun to Mitchell in the corner of the end zone.

"Where else would you rather be?" Bennett said of his final offensive drive. "Having the ball with two minutes left, and if you score a touchdown, you win the game. I looked around, and there were a whole bunch of determined, strong stares from all the dudes. It gave me confidence."

When Coach Kirby Smart's team won the national title a year ago, the Bulldogs ended a 41-year title drought, and now they have a chance to repeat as champions. Georgia will face No. 3 TCU in the national title game on Jan. 9 at SoFi Stadium in Inglewood, Calif. If the Bulldogs win there, it would serve as the ultimate career ending for Bennett, the former scout team quarterback who transferred away, then returned as a scholarship player and spent years climbing the depth chart.

The No. 4 Buckeyes challenged Georgia, pushing the Bulldogs into their largest deficit of the season when they twice trailed by 14 points. Georgia made mistakes and struggled to contain Stroud all evening. Bennett, who threw an interception in the second quarter, said he "felt like there was a 30-minute period there where I just played bad football." The Bulldogs logged only 32 yards during the third quarter, a dreary stretch in which the win drifted further from reach.

But during Georgia's final three drives, when the team mustered a field goal and two touchdowns to climb out of the two-score hole, Bennett's offense tallied 210 yards. That burst required a key fourth-down completion from star tight end Brock Bowers, initially

Bulldogs receiver Adonai Mitchell (5) celebrates after a 10-yard touchdown catch to give his team the lead in the fourth quarter of a 42-41 win over Ohio State in the Peach Bowl.

ruled short of the line to gain but overturned upon review. Smart later called a timeout just before Ohio State snapped what would have been a successful fake punt with about nine minutes to go. Smart described the decision as "one of those gut reactions." He said he "didn't think that we had it lined up properly to stop it," and it proved to be a critical move.

Eventually, Bennett, the 25-year-old quarterback, completed all five of his pass attempts on his team's final series, punctuated by the grab from Mitchell, who had been injured during the season and entered this matchup with his most recent reception coming in September.

The undefeated Bulldogs looked invincible through much of this season, previously winning games by an average of 26 points, but Stroud and his elite receivers posed a difficult task. Stroud threw for 348 yards and four touchdowns as he picked apart Georgia's struggling secondary.

"On the biggest stage," Coach Ryan Day said, "[Stroud] played one of his best games."

Marvin Harrison Jr., a sophomore but already one of the best receivers in the country, grabbed two of Stroud's touchdown passes in the first half as the Buckeyes surged ahead, and teammate Emeka Egbuka combined with Harrison to make Ohio State's passing attack an unstoppable force. These receivers, plus Stroud's savvy, are the engines of the Buckeyes' offense, and they thrived against the best defense they had faced all season.

Marvin Harrison Jr., a sophomore but already one of the best receivers in the country, grabbed two of Stroud's touchdown passes in the first half as the Buckeyes surged ahead, and teammate Emeka Egbuka

Adonai Mitchell makes the game-winning touchdown catch in the end zone against Ohio State in the Peach Bowl.

combined with Harrison to make Ohio State's passing attack an unstoppable force. These receivers, plus Stroud's savvy, are the engines of the Buckeyes' offense, and they thrived against the best defense they had faced all season.

"Those guys made plays when they needed to make plays," Georgia defensive back Javon Bullard said of Ohio State's offensive playmakers. "We knew coming into the game, it wouldn't be perfect."

The Buckeyes lost Harrison when he was ruled out late in the third quarter because of concussion protocols. On a third-down play, Harrison took a hard hit in the back of the end zone from Bullard that was reviewed for targeting but didn't lead to a penalty. Ohio State settled for a field goal that extended its advantage to 38-24.

Then Georgia's fourth-quarter resurgence began. The Bulldogs eventually trimmed Ohio State's comfortable lead to 38-35 with Arian Smith's 76-yard touchdown grab and a successful pass to Ladd McConkey on a two-point conversion. With 8:41 left in the game, Stroud and the offense took the field but couldn't reach the end zone. Ruggles hit a 48-yard field goal to give the Buckeyes a precarious six-point lead. And Bennett pounced on the opportunity.

Ohio State backed into the playoff. The last time the Buckeyes took the field, they looked vulnerable, with Michigan pummeling them in the fourth quarter. That lopsided defeat in late November forced Ohio State's players to stay home during conference championship weekend, then rely on Southern California's blowout loss in the Pac-12 title game to earn a playoff berth.

Despite the flaws exposed by Ohio State's archrival, particularly its defense allowing explosive plays, the Buckeyes have one of

Georgia receiver Arian Smith makes an uncontested catch against Ohio State.

the few rosters in the country that can match up with Georgia's talent. Both programs reside on an exclusive tier in which five-star prospects flock to campus each year and their brands pique the interest of recruits nationwide. Those players gave Ohio State a chance — and the ability to hold a lead through much of the game — but Georgia prevailed.

After ending the program's title drought last year, the Bulldogs returned with force this season. They stormed through what was supposed to be a difficult opener against Oregon, then their conference slate and the SEC title game. But what matters most is their next game, because this season will ultimately be remembered as one that ended with another national title or a year the Bulldogs fell short.

Georgia quarterback Stetson Bennett runs into the end zone for a second-quarter touchdown against Ohio State.

Bulldogs defensive back Javon Bullard sacks Ohio State quarterback C.J. Stroud during the third quarter.

Bulldogs receiver Arian Smith celebrates after making a touchdown catch against Ohio State.

#	Name	Pos.	Ht.	Wt.	Year	Hometown
0	Rian Davis	LB	6'-2"	230	JR	Apopka, FL
0	Darnell Washington	TE	6'-7"	270	JR	Las Vegas, NV
1	Nyland Green	DB	6'-1"	185	FR	Covington, GA
1	Marcus Rosemy-Jacksaint	WR	6'-2"	195	JR	Pompano Beach, FL
2	Kendall Milton	RB	6'-1"	220	JR	Fresno, CA
2	Smael Mondon Jr.	LB	6'-3"	220	SO	Dallas, GA
3	Kamari Lassiter	DB	6'-0"	180	SO	Savannah, GA
3	Andrew Paul	RB	5'-11"	220	FR	Dallas, TX
4	Oscar Delp	TE	6'-5"	225	FR	Cumming, GA
4	Nolan Smith	LB	6'-3"	235	SR	Savannah, GA
5	Adonai Mitchell	WR	6'-4"	190	SO	Missouri City, TX
5	Kelee Ringo	DB	6'-2"	210	SO	Tacoma, WA
6	Daylen Everette	DB	6'-1"	190	FR	Norfolk, VA
6	Kenny McIntosh	RB	6'-1"	210	SR	Fort Lauderdale, FL
7	Arik Gilbert	TE	6'-5"	255	SO	Marietta, GA
7	Marvin Jones Jr.	LB	6'-5"	250	FR	Sunrise, FL
8	Dominick Blaylock	WR	6'-1"	205	JR	Marietta, GA
8	MJ Sherman	LB	6'-2"	250	JR	Baltimore, MD
9	Jackson Meeks	WR	6'-2"	205	SO	Phenix City, AL
9	Jaheim Singletary	DB	6'-1"	175	FR	Jacksonville, FL
10	Jamon Dumas-Johnson	LB	6'-1"	245	SO	Hyattsville, MD
10	Kearis Jackson	WR	6'-0"	200	SR	Fort Valley, GA
11	Arian Smith	WR	6'-0"	185	SO	Bradley, FL
11	Jalon Walker	LB	6'-2"	225	FR	Salisbury, NC
12	Julian Humphrey	DB	6'-0"	190	FR	Webster, TX
12	Brock Vandagriff	QB	6'-3"	205	FR	Bogart, GA
13	Stetson Bennett	QB	5'-11"	190	SR	Blackshear, GA
13	Mykel Williams	DL	6'-5"	265	FR	Columbus, GA
14	David Daniel-Sisavanh	DB	6'-2"	185	SO	Woodstock, GA
14	Gunner Stockton	QB	6'-1"	210	FR	Tiger, GA
15	Carson Beck	QB	6'-4"	215	SO	Jacksonville, FL
15	Trezmen Marshall	LB	6'-1"	230	JR	Homerville, GA
16	C.J. Madden	DE	6'-4"	230	FR	Ellenwood, GA
16	Jackson Muschamp	QB	6'-2"	190	SO	Columbia, SC
17	Dan Jackson	DB	6'-1"	190	JR	Gainesville, GA
18	C.J. Smith	WR	6'-3"	175	FR	Apopka, FL
18	Xavian Sorey Jr.	LB	6'-3"	214	FR	Campbellton, FL
19	Brock Bowers	TE	6'-4"	230	SO	Napa, CA
19	Darris Smith	LB	6'-5"	225	FR	Baxley, GA
20	Sevaughn Clark	RB	6'-1"	215	JR	Dawsonville, GA
20	JaCorey Thomas	DB	6'-0"	200	FR	Orlando, FL
22	Javon Bullard	DB	5'-11"	180	SO	Milledgeville, GA
22	Branson Robinson	RB	5'-10"	220	FR	Canton, MS
23	De'Nylon Morrissette	WR	6'-1"	200	FR	Stone Mountain, GA
23	Tykee Smith	DB	5'-10"	198	JR	Philadelphia, PA
24	Nathan Priestley	WR	6'-4"	205	JR	Los Angeles, CA
24	Malaki Starks	DB	6'-1"	205	FR	Jefferson, GA
25	E.J. Lightsey	LB	6'-2"	223	FR	Fitzgerald, GA
26	Collin Drake	QB	6'-1"	195	FR	Ennis, TX
27	C.J. Washington	LB	6'-1"	220	FR	Cedartown, GA
28	Marcus Washington Jr.	DB	6'-1"	185	FR	Grovetown, GA
29	Luke Bennett	WR	5'-11"	175	FR	Blackshear, GA
29	Christopher Smith	DB	5'-11"	195	SR	Atlanta, GA
30	Daijun Edwards	RB	5'-10"	201	JR	Norman Park, GA
30	Terrell Foster	LB	6'-1"	210	FR	Kennesaw, GA
31	Grant Briscoe	WR	6'-3"	190	FR	Carrollton, GA
31	William Poole	DB	6'-0"	190	SR	Atlanta, GA
32	Chaz Chambliss	LB	6'-2"	250	SO	Carrollton, GA
32	Cash Jones	RB	6'-0"	182	FR	Brock, TX
33	Robert Beal Jr.	LB	6'-4"	250	SR	Duluth, GA
35	Jacob Fleming	S	5'-11"	190	FR	Atlanta, GA
36	Randon Jernigan	WR	6'-0"	183	SR	Brunswick, GA
36	Colby Smith	DB	5'-10"	170	SO	Danielsville, GA
37	Drew Southern	DB	5'-11"	180	FR	Cumming, GA
38	Brooks Bortle	WR	6'-1"	185	FR	Roswell, GA
38	Patrick Taylor	DB	6'-0"	175	SO	Johns Creek, GA
39	Parker Jones	WR	5'-11"	165	FR	Albany, GA
39	Miles Thornton	WR	6'-0"	190	FR	Tyrone, GA
41	Denton Shamburger	DE	6'-0"	175	FR	Atlanta, GA
42	Graham Collins	LB	6'-2"	215	SO	Atlanta, GA
43	Davis Day	TE	6'-4"	240	SR	Hamilton, GA
44	Cade Brock	TE	6'-0"	250	SO	Subligna, GA
45	Jacob Hardie	RB	5'-9"	180	FR	Olney, MD
45	Bill Norton	DL	6'-6"	300	JR	Memphis, TN
46	Payton Bowles	DB	5'-10"	170	SO	Athens, GA
46	George Vining	WR	6'-0"	205	SR	Macon, GA
47	Payne Walker	LS	6'-2"	249	SR	Suwanee, GA
48	Joseph Daniels	DB	5'-10"	188	SR	Johns Creek, GA
48	Cooper Johnson	TE	6'-4"	220	FR	Cumming, GA
49	Samuel Johnson	TE	6'-1"	230	FR	Lilburn, GA
49	Jamier Moten	DB	5'-8"	160	FR	Charlotte, NC
50	Warren Ericson	OL	6'-4"	305	SR	Suwanee, GA
52	Christen Miller	DL	6'-4"	295	FR	Ellenwood, GA
53	Dylan Fairchild	OL	6'-5"	300	FR	Cumming, GA
55	Jared Wilson	OL	6'-3"	300	FR	Winston-salem, NC
56	Micah Morris	OL	6'-6"	330	FR	Kingsland, GA
56	William Mote	LS	6'-2"	230	JR	Hoover, AL
57	Luke Collins	LB	6'-2"	245	FR	Birmingham, AL
58	Austin Blaske	OL	6'-5"	310	SO	Bloomingdale, GA
59	Broderick Jones	OL	6'-4"	310	SO	Lithonia, GA
63	Sedrick Van Pran	OL	6'-4"	310	SO	New Orleans, LA
64	Jacob Hood	OL	6'-8"	350	FR	Nashville, TN
65	Amarius Mims	OL	6'-7"	330	SO	Cochran, GA
66	Aliou Bah	OL	6'-5"	330	FR	Memphis, TN
66	Jonathan Washburn	LS	6'-2"	230	FR	Ringgold, GA
68	Chris Brown	OL	6'-5"	315	SO	Savannah, GA
69	Tate Ratledge	OL	6'-6"	315	SO	Rome, GA
70	Warren McClendon	OL	6'-4"	300	JR	Brunswick, GA
71	Earnest Greene III	OL	6'-4"	330	FR	Los Angeles, CA
72	Griffin Scroggs	OL	6'-3"	315	FR	Grayson, GA
73	Xavier Truss	OL	6'-7"	320	JR	West Warwick, RI
74	Drew Bobo	OL	6'-5"	290	FR	Auburn, AL
76	Miles Johnson	OL	6'-5"	320	SO	Blue Ridge, GA
77	Devin Willock	OL	6'-7"	335	SO	New Milford, NJ
78	Chad Lindberg	OL	6'-6"	325	SO	League City, TX
78	Nazir Stackhouse	DL	6'-3"	320	JR	Stone Mountain, GA
79	Weston Wallace	OL	6'-4"	320	SO	Eatonton, GA
80	Brett Seither	TE	6'-5"	228	JR	Clearwater, FL
82	Logan Johnson	WR	5'-6"	155	FR	Bogart, GA
83	Cole Speer	WR	5'-11"	185	FR	Calhoun, GA
84	Ladd McConkey	WR	6'-0"	185	SO	Chatsworth, GA
85	Drew Sheehan	TE	6'-2"	215	JR	Woodstock, GA
86	Dillon Bell	WR	6'-1"	210	FR	Houston, TX
87	Mekhi Mews	WR	5'-8"	170	FR	Grayson, GA
88	Jalen Carter	DL	6'-3"	300	JR	Apopka, FL
88	Ryland Goede	TE	6'-6"	240	JR	Kennesaw, GA
89	Braxton Hicks	WR	6'-2"	195	SO	Tiger, GA
90	Tramel Walthour	DL	6'-3"	280	SR	Hinesville, GA
92	Brett Thorson	P	6'-2"	210	FR	Melbourne, VIC
93	Tyrion Ingram-Dawkins	DL	6'-5"	300	FR	Gaffney, SC
94	Henry Bates	K	5'-11"	170	FR	Waycross, GA
94	Jonathan Jefferson	DL	6'-3"	295	FR	Douglasville, GA
95	Shone Washington	DL	6'-4"	270	FR	New Orleans, LA
96	Zion Logue	DL	6'-5"	295	JR	Lebanon, TN
96	Jack Podlesny	K	6'-1"	180	SR	Saint Simons Island, GA
97	Warren Brinson	DL	6'-4"	305	JR	Savannah, GA
97	Matthew Sumlin	K	5'-11"	170	SO	Smyrna, GA
98	Noah Jones	P	6'-0"	165	FR	Cairo, GA
99	Bear Alexander	DL	6'-3"	305	FR	Denton, TX
99	Jared Zirkel	K	6'-3"	185	SO	Kerrville, TX